j
428.1
R27au

Animals
UP
and
DOWN

LASELL COLLEGE LIBRARY
80A Maple St.
Auburndale, MA 02466

amicus
readers

Mankato, Minnesota

by Beth Bence Reinke

Ideas for Parents and Teachers

Amicus Readers let children practice reading informational texts at the earliest reading levels. Familiar words and concepts with close photo-text matches support early readers.

Before Reading

- Discuss the cover photo with the child. What does it tell him?
- Ask the child to predict what she will learn in the book.

Read the Book

- "Walk" through the book and look at the photos. Let the child ask questions.
- Read the book to the child, or have the child read independently.

After Reading

- Use the photo quiz at the end of the book to review the text.
- Prompt the child to make connections. Ask: *Can you think of other animals that are up or down?*

Amicus Readers are published by Amicus
P.O. Box 1329, Mankato, MN 56002
www.amicuspublishing.us

Copyright © 2014. International copyright reserved in all countries. No part of this book may be reproduced in any form without written permission from the publisher.

Library of Congress Cataloging-in-Publication Data

Reinke, Beth Bence.
  Animals up and down / Beth Bence Reinke.
    pages cm. -- (Animal Antonyms)
  ISBN 978-1-60753-500-3 (hardcover) -- ISBN 978-1-60753-535-5 (eBook)
  1. English language--Synonyms and antonyms--Juvenile literature. 2. English language--Comparison--Juvenile literature. 3. Animals--Juvenile literature. I. Title.
  PE1591.R468 2014
  428.1--dc23
                        2013004512

Photo Credits: Rich Carey/Shutterstock Images, cover (bottom); Steve Collender/Shutterstock Images, cover (top front); Adrian Nunez/ Shutterstock Images, cover (top back); Eric Gevaert/Shutterstock Images, 1 (top); Ron Rowan Photography/Shutterstock Images, 1 (bottom), 16 (bottom middle); Sebastian Knight/Shutterstock Images, 3 (top), 16 (bottom right); Kristina Vackova/ Shutterstock Images, 3 (bottom); Igor Kovalenko/ Shutterstock Images, 4, 16 (top left); Natursports/ Shutterstock Images, 5, 16 (top middle); Worldswildlifewonders/Shutterstock Images, 6; Margaret M Stewart/Shutterstock Images, 7, 16 (bottom left); Jiri Foltyn/Shutterstock Images, 8, 16 (top right); Jupiterimages/Thinkstock, 9; EcoPrint/ Shutterstock Images, 10, 12; Hung Chung Chih/ Shutterstock Images, 11; BMJ/Shutterstock Images, 13; Sokolov Alexey/Shutterstock Images, 14; Willyam Bradberry/Shutterstock Images, 15

Produced for Amicus by The Peterson Publishing Company and Red Line Editorial

Editor Jenna Gleisner
Designer Jake Nordby
Printed in the United States of America
Mankato, MN
July, 2013
PA 1938
10 9 8 7 6 5 4 3 2 1

Up and down are antonyms. Antonyms are words that are opposites. Which animals are up or down?

Eagles fly high up
in the air.

Fish swim deep down
in the ocean.

Red-eyed tree frogs climb up into trees to stay safe.

Chipmunks dash
down into burrows
to stay safe.

Elephants lift their trunks
up in the air. They spray
water up when they take
a bath.

Anteaters dig their
snouts down into logs.
They catch ants with
their sticky tongues.

Meerkats stand up on their hind legs to watch for danger.

Otters slide down into water to swim and look for food.

Rhinoceros horns point up. Rhinos can charge at lions with their horns.

Walrus tusks point down.
Tusks help walruses climb
onto the ice.

Some animals can be up
and down. Dolphins swim
up for air.

They dive back down into
the sea and swim away.

Photo Quiz

Which animals are up?
Which animals are down?